To Scott

Welsh
It's Wales

Dishes

Rhian Williams

y Lolfa

First impression: April 2000
Second impression: 2002

© Copyright Rhian Williams and Y Lolfa Cyf., 2000

Cover design: Ceri Jones
Cover photograph: Robat Gruffudd

ISBN: 0 86243 492 0

Printed, on acid free and partly recycled paper
and published and bound in Wales by:
Y Lolfa Cyf., Talybont, Ceredigion SY24 5AP
e-mail ylolfa@ylolfa.com
internet http://www.ylolfa.com/
phone +44 (0)1970 832 304
fax 832 782
isdn 832 813

Contents

Introduction

The traditional cooking of the Welsh, Irish and Scots have several similarities. The ingredients that they used were either grown, collected or caught locally. Hardly anything was bought except tea, sugar, salt and spices. Their methods of cooking were also similar, mostly in a pot or on a bakestone on an open hearth. Their fires were heated by peat, the basic fuel for poor people for many centuries. The dishes themselves were simple fare, prepared by frugal but imaginative housewives. These recipes were handed down from mothers to daughters over many years and Welsh Cakes are a classic example.

At times it must have been quite a struggle for the women to find enough food for all the family, when we remember that most families were quite large. I love the story about Beti Jones in the book *Cwm Eithin* by Hugh Evans. Poor old Beti had a large brood. I think that she had twenty-five children. As you can imagine, meal-times must have been pretty chaotic – mainly moans and groans about what food they liked and disliked. One day, she decided to let each child choose his or her own meal. When the food was ready she emptied each dish into a large pan and mixed it all together. Then each child had to eat from the pan, and none of the children could leave the table until the pan was empty. Each meal was peaceful for Beti after that. What a lovely trick she had played on them!

Some of the following recipes are old and reliable friends, but there is also an opportunity to make new friends.

RHIAN WILLIAMS
April 2000

Vegetable and Cheese Recipes
Ryseitiau Llysiau a Chaws

Welsh Rarebit
Caws Blasus

**Was this dish once called Welsh Rabbit or Welsh Rarebit?
I've never found out.**

4 slices of thin bread without the crusts
2 ozs (50g) butter
8 ozs (225g) cheddar cheese
¼ pint (150ml) milk
1 level teaspoon mustard powder
1 egg, well beaten

Melt the butter in a heavy saucepan, then add the cheese and milk. Stir continuously until soft and smooth. Add the egg and mustard powder.

Toast the bread until golden brown on both sides. Stir the mixture well – do not allow it to boil or it will become stringy.

Pour over the toasts and serve at once. Sprinkle with salt and pepper to taste.

Caerphilly Salad
Salad Caerffili

The flaky texture of the cheese makes this an interesting salad.

1 small or large lettuce
5 fl ozs (142ml) soured cream
3 tablespoons milk
1 teaspoon lemon juice
1 level teaspoon caster sugar
pinch of salt
2 medium eating apples, peeled and diced
8 ozs (225g) diced Caerphilly cheese
1 small tin of pineapple rings, drained and cubed
2 teaspoons chopped parsley

Wash, dry and cut the lettuce into fairly small pieces. Place on the bottom of a salad bowl. Mix the cream, milk, lemon juice, sugar and salt in a bowl. Add the apples, cheese and pineapple and mix well. Spread over the lettuce and sprinkle with parsley.

Anglesey Eggs
Wyau Sir Fôn

My father's family came from Anglesey and each time he went to visit them he came home laden with eggs. It was after such a visit that we had fluffy golden omelettes.

1 medium cauliflower
4 eggs
1½ ozs (40g) butter
1½ ozs (40g) plain flour
¾ pint (400ml) milk
salt and pepper
4 ozs (125g) grated cheese

Prepare the cauliflower by cutting off the florets and washing them in cold water. Cook in salted water for 20 minutes, then drain. Meanwhile, hard-boil the eggs and remove the shells. Melt the butter in a saucepan and add the flour, stirring continuously until the mixture has thickened. Add the milk a little at a time, bring to the boil, add seasoning and 3 ozs (75g) of the cheese. Place the cauliflower in an ovenproof dish. Cut the eggs into quarters and place around the dish. Cover evenly with the sauce. Sprinkle the rest of the cheese on top and place under the grill until golden brown.

Leek Pie
Pastai Cennin

I have read that St David loved to eat leeks. If so, he would really have enjoyed this dish.

Pastry case:
6 ozs (175g) plain flour
3 ozs (75g) fat
pinch of salt
water to mix

Filling:
3 medium-sized leeks
1 tablespoon plain flour, seasoned with a little salt and pepper
4 ozs (125g) grated cooking cheese
2 tablespoons milk
1 beaten egg

Rub the fat into the flour and salt, then add enough water to form a dough. Prepare the leeks and cut them into ½" (1.2 cm) pieces, parboil in a little salted water and drain. Roll out half the pastry and line a shallow 7" (18 cm) pie dish with it. Roll out the remainder of the pastry and cut into ¾" (2 cm) strips. Place the leeks into the pie dish and sprinkle with the seasoned flour. Mix the cheese with the milk and spread evenly on the leeks. Use the pastry strips to make a lattice on top. Glaze with the beaten egg and bake at 220°C/425°F/gas mark 7 for 30 minutes.

Baked Onions
Wynwyn Wedi'u Pobi

A warming dish on a cold winter's day.

4 large onions
2 ozs (50g) minced meat
2 ozs (50g) breadcrumbs
I oz (25g) butter
salt and pepper

Peel the onions and boil in salted water for about 15 minutes. Drain and leave to cool a little.

Cook the meat in butter with salt and pepper, then drain well. Remove the centre of each onion with a sharp knife. Mix with the meat, breadcrumbs, salt and pepper. Fill the centre of the onions with the mixture. Place the onions on a greased baking tin and top them with a little butter. Bake at 180°C/350°F/gas mark 5 for 30 minutes. Serve with crisp rolls and cheese.

Quarryman's Supper
Tatws Pum Munud

The men who worked in the North Wales quarries used to walk from Anglesey and the Lleyn Peninsula. They came to work on Sunday evening and returned home on Saturday afternoon. They stayed in the Barracks and fended for themselves. My grandfather was one of them. This is one of the dishes they made in a frying pan – it was supposed to be cooked in five minutes. I cook it in an ovenproof dish.

1 large onion
2 lbs (900g) potatoes
1 oz (25g) plain flour
6 rashers of bacon
½ pint (300ml) hot water
salt and pepper
2 meat stock cubes

Peel the onions and potatoes and slice thinly. Take the rind off the bacon and cut each rasher in half. Grease an ovenproof dish and place layers of onion, bacon and potato alternately, ending with potato.

Dissolve the stock cubes in the water, add salt and pepper. Make the flour into a paste with a little cold water. Add to the beef stock, mix well and pour into the ovenproof dish. Bake for 1¼ hours at 180°C/350°F/gas mark 5.

Swede, Parsnips and Beetroot
Rwdan, Pannas a Bitrwt

These were the basic winter vegetables for the ordinary people of Wales in the past and many housewives tried to make them more interesting. Potatoes were used throughout the year, with onions, leeks and carrots being used in casseroles and stews.

Swede Bake
Rwdan yn y Popty

2 ozs (50g) butter
I large onion
6 rindless rashers of bacon
6 ozs (175g) of mushrooms
I oz (25g) of plain flour
½ pint (300ml) of beef stock
I lb (450g) swede
salt and pepper
I crushed clove of garlic

Peel and chop the onion and mushrooms. Cut the bacon into small pieces, peel and slice the swede. Melt 1 oz (25g) of the butter, add the onion, bacon and garlic. Stir and cook for 5 minutes. Add the mushrooms and cook for a further 5 minutes. Sprinkle the flour over and cook for 1 minute, stirring continuously and adding the stock slowly.

Place a layer of swede on the bottom of a greased ovenproof dish. Spread the mixture on top and cover with the rest of the swede. Sprinkle with salt and pepper and the remainder of the butter cut into small pieces. Bake for 1 hour, or until the swede is cooked, at 180°C/350°F/gas mark 5.

Parsnip Soup
Cawl Pannas

1 oz (25g) butter
1 large onion – peeled and sliced
1lb (450g) parsnips – peeled and cut into small pieces
¼ teaspoon ginger powder
1 pint (600 ml) chicken stock – made from two chicken-flavoured
stock cubes
salt and pepper
¼ pint (150ml) single cream

Melt the butter in a pan, add the parsnips and onions and cook for 5 minutes, stirring continuously. Add the stock and seasoning, simmer for 1 hour. Leave to cool a little and put in a blender or through a sieve. Taste, adding more seasoning if necessary. Place the mixture in a pan and heat, being sure not to allow it to boil. Pour into soup dishes and swirl a little cream on top.

Hot Beetroot
Bitrwt Poeth

½ oz (15g) butter
2 tablespoons chopped onions
2 ozs (50g) sugar
½ oz (15g) cornflour
½ teaspoon salt
5 tablespoons vinegar
1½ lbs (700g) cooked, cubed beetroot

Melt the butter in a pan and cook the onions until tender. Mix in the sugar, cornflour, salt and vinegar, stirring continuously until the mixture thickens. Add the beetroot and stir well until it is hot, but do not allow it to boil. Serve with cold meat and fresh bread.

Laver Bread
Bara Lawr

South Wales is well-known for its laver bread. It is made from laver, an edible seaweed and an excellent source of vitamins. The first time I had some, it had been made into little cakes. These had been fried and they were served with bacon. I had my doubts about them, but I found them very tasty.

4 ozs (125g) prepared laver bread
1 oz (25g) medium/fine oatmeal
1 egg
a little plain flour
bacon fat or butter to fry

Beat the egg, mix with the laver bread and oatmeal. Form into about 6 balls, roll them in the flour and flatten into little cakes. Fry in the fat, turn over once and serve with bacon and eggs.

Coleslaw
Salad Bresych

Bought coleslaw is quite nice, but one which has been made at home is far better.

1 medium carrot

1 small onion

4 celery stalks

1lb (450g) white cabbage

2 tablespoons (30ml) vegetable oil

1 tablespoon (15ml) ordinary vinegar

1oz (25g) granulated sugar

1 tablespoon (15ml) mayonnaise

5 fl oz (150ml) fresh single cream

A little salt and pepper

Peel the carrot and onion and wash the celery well. Shred the cabbage, grate the onion and carrot and chop the celery. Mix them together and add the rest of the ingredients with salt and pepper to taste. Mix well and leave in a cool place for twelve hours or overnight. Mix again before serving.

Fish and Meat Recipes
Ryseitiau Pysgod a Chig

Pembroke Cockles
Cocos Penfro

Cardiff market has an excellent fish stall and, of course, cockles can be bought there as in most fish shops in Wales. The cockles are at their best in the winter, and the traditional way to eat them is with salt, vinegar, bread and butter. Why not give this recipe a try?

2 dozen fresh cockles
2 ozs (50g) oatmeal
1 oz (25g) plain flour
3 tablespoons oil
2 ozs (50g) butter

Wash and drain the cockles. Mix the oatmeal and flour together and put into a plastic food bag. Put about four cockles into the bag and shake well to coat each cockle evenly. Repeat until all the cockles are coated. Melt the oil and butter together, stir until the fat is hot. Fry each cockle in the fat until golden brown. Serve hot with salt and vinegar.

Nefyn Herrings
Penwaig Nefyn

As Wales has an abundance of seashores, lakes and rivers, fish has always been an important part of the diet of the Welsh people. I love herrings cooked in this way – the bones become so soft that they cause no problems.

4 herrings
1 medium onion – finely chopped
salt and pepper
½ teaspoon mustard powder
¼ pint (150 ml) water
2 ozs (50g) plain flour

Cut the head, tail and fins off the herrings. Clean the insides and wash well. Grease an ovenproof dish. Mix the flour, salt, pepper and mustard powder and coat the herrings – inside and out – with the mixture. Place them in the dish and sprinkle with the onion. Mix the vinegar and water and pour over the herrings. Cover the dish and bake at 180°C/350°F/gas mark 5 for 2 – 2½ hours. Serve hot or cold.

Baked Mackerel
Mecryll Wedi'u Pobi

**I like mackerel when they have been coated with plain flour
and fried. However, baked mackerel are also very tasty.
Why not try them?**

4 large mackerel
1 oz (25g) suet
4 ozs (125g) bacon
2 ozs (50g) breadcrumbs
1 oz (25g) butter
1 egg
2 teaspoons chopped parsley
salt and pepper

Mix all the dry ingredients together and bind with the beaten egg. Prepare the
fish by removing the head, tail and fins. Clean them and take out the backbone
– smaller bones do not matter. Divide the stuffing between the fish and place
them in a greased dish with a little butter on each. Sprinkle the parsley on top
and cover. Bake at 180°C/350°F/gas mark 5 for about 2 hours.

Llanfair Fish
Pysgod Llanfair

This dish can be prepared using most fish – provided there are not too many bones! Fish such as cod, hake, haddock or tuna are fine.

1 lb (450g) cooked fish
1 oz (25g) butter
1 oz (25g) plain flour
½ pint (300ml) milk
salt and pepper
2 ozs (50g) grated cheese
3 medium tomatoes

Remove the skin and bones from the fish and flake it. Melt the butter on a low heat, mix in the flour and stir continuously. When the mixture has thickened add the milk a little at a time. Bring to the boil. Add salt and pepper to taste. Mix in ¾ of the cheese, add the fish and mix well. Place in an ovenproof dish and sprinkle the rest of the cheese on top. Slice the tomatoes and place on the grated cheese. Bake at 180°C/350°F/gas mark 5 for 30 minutes or until crisp and brown.

Lobscouse and Cawl
Lobscows a Chawl

Lobscouse and Cawl are quite similar in as much as they are thick broths made from meat and vegetables. I wonder if they are North Wales and South Wales versions of the same dish? This may be so, but each has a very different taste. We have both in our house and I am sure that they would both be welcomed after a rugby match.

Lobscouse
Lobscows

When I was young we had this during the week and with luck there would be enough for two days. If there was only a little left my mother would sieve it all and add more water and a beef cube to make a soup. Then we would have fruit pie and custard to follow – wonderful!

a piece of brisket or shin, about 2 lbs (900g)
2 lbs (900g) potatoes
1 lb (450g) carrots
1 large onion
1 small swede
1 large tablespoon split peas, pre-soaked
salt and pepper
water

Place the meat in a large pan after removing excess fat. Prepare all the vegetables and cut into small pieces. Place in the pan and add the split peas. Cover with water and add salt and pepper. Bring to the boil and simmer gently until the meat is cooked – 2 hours or more, but be careful not to let it boil dry. Taste, adding more seasoning if needed. Serve in soup dishes with plenty of fresh bread.

Cawl

Cawl

My husband prepares this and it is always excellent.

a piece of ham, mutton or shin, about 2 lbs (900g)
1 lb (450g) onions
1 lb (450g) leeks
1 lb (450g) carrots
1 small swede
2 lbs (900g) potatoes
1 heaped tablespoon split peas, pre-soaked
salt and pepper
water

Remove excess fat from the meat and cut into small pieces. Place in a large saucepan and cover with water. Add salt and pepper. Prepare all the vegetables by peeling and cutting into cubes or small pieces. Add to the saucepan with the split peas and bring to the boil. Simmer for 1½ – 2 hours. Taste and add more seasoning if needed.

Rissoles
Teisennau Cig

A handy and tasty way of using leftover lamb – or any other meat.

½ lb (250g) cooked minced meat
1 oz (25g) butter or margarine
1 tablespoon chopped onion
1 oz (25g) plain flour
¼ pint (150ml) stock or a little leftover gravy
salt and pepper
1 tablespoon chopped parsley
1 beaten egg

Melt the fat in a saucepan and add the onion; fry gently until cooked. Add the flour and stir until the mixture has thickened. Pour in the stock or gravy and cook well, stirring continuously. Add the meat, parsley and seasoning. Mix well and turn onto a plate, flatten out and leave to cool. Divide into 6 – 8 portions and form into rounds. Coat each with egg and breadcrumbs, then fry until golden brown on both sides. Drain well and serve hot.

Gwynedd Lamb
Oen Gwynedd

This dish takes time to prepare and cook, but it is well worth the effort.

2 lbs (900g) thick slices of lamb or lamb chops
1 meat stock cube dissolved in ½ pint (300ml) hot water
1 lb (450g) carrots
1 medium leek
1 large onion
salt and pepper
oil

Prepare the meat by removing excess fat. Fry in the oil until golden brown on both sides. Prepare all the vegetables and cut into small pieces. Place the meat in an ovenproof dish, add the vegetables, stock, salt and pepper. Cover and bake at 180°C/350°F/gas mark 5 for 2 hours or until the meat is tender. Serve with fluffy mashed potatoes and garden peas.

Chicken with Honey
Cyw Iâr a Mêl

The honey gives this dish a pleasant but unusual flavour. It is ideal if you are expecting guests, but do not know exactly what time they will arrive!

3 ozs (75g) margarine
2 medium onions, finely chopped
1 large tin chopped tomatoes
1 tablespoon brown sauce
2 tablespoons soft honey
salt and pepper
5 ozs (150g) long grain rice
6 chicken pieces, thighs or drumsticks

Put the chicken pieces in the oven. Bake at 180°C/350°F/gas mark 5 for 45 minutes. Cook the onion, tomatoes, brown sauce, honey, salt and pepper in the margarine for 30 minutes. Boil the rice in salted water, drain and place on the bottom of a serving dish – if the meal is to be kept warm use an ovenproof dish. Place the pieces of chicken on top and cover with the sauce.

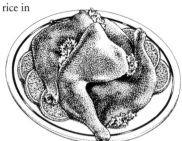

Oven Baked Chicken
Cyw Iâr yn y Popty

This used to be made with older, tougher birds, but all chickens are tender these days.

4 pieces of chicken
seasoned flour
2 tablespoons cooking oil
1 large onion
½ lb (225g) shelled peas
½ lb (225g) carrots
2 ozs (50g) long grain rice
salt and pepper
½ pint (300ml) chicken stock – a chicken-flavoured stock cube can be used

Dip the chicken pieces in the seasoned flour, cover well and fry in the oil until golden brown on both sides. Meanwhile, dice the carrots and onions and slice the tomatoes. Mix the vegetables, adding salt and pepper for seasoning. Place the mixture at the bottom of an ovenproof dish and put the chicken pieces on top. Mix the rice with the stock and pour into the dish. Cover and bake at 180°C/350°F/gas mark 5 for 1½ – 2 hours.

Fish Pie
Pastai Bysgod

Although it is good value for money, fish can be expensive. It is no longer a cheap dish, and I doubt whether, in the olden days, the housewives of Wales could afford to buy it at prices relative to those of today. This dish has two good points. It makes a small amount of fish go a long way, and it can be prepared the day before.

1lb (450g) white fish
½ pint (300ml) milk
1 medium onion, chopped
a bunch of herbs in a muslin bag
salt and pepper
2lbs (900g) potatoes, boiled and mashed
2 large tomatoes
1 oz (25g) butter
1oz (25g) plain flour
3 oz (75g) grated cheese

Place the fish in a saucepan with the milk, butter, chopped onion, herbs and a little salt and pepper. Simmer gently for 15 minutes or until the fish has cooked. Place the mashed potatoes on the bottom of a greased casserole dish. Remove any bones or skin from the fish and place it on top of the potatoes. Slice the tomatoes and place on the fish. Remove the herbs from the pan and make the liquid up to half a pint with water, then add the butter. Mix the flour with a little water to make a smooth paste. Add to the liquid and onions and bring to the boil, stirring continuously. When the sauce has thickened, pour it evenly over the tomatoes. Cover with the cheese and bake at 180°C/350°F/gas mark 5 for 1 hour.

Beuno Pork
Porc Beuno

I think that pork, not lamb, should be the traditional Welsh meat. Pigs have been very important in the life of the Welsh people for hundreds of years. They are mentioned in the 'Mabinogi' – the story of 'Y Twrch Trwyth', also in such place names as Nant y Moch. Why, then, is lamb more popular? It could be due to the taste – pork can be very bland. However, this recipe is very tasty.

1lb (500g) fillet of pork
1 oz (25g) plain flour
2 oz (50g) butter
2 tablespoons (30ml) tomato sauce
¼ pint (150ml) stock – a dissolved meat cube could be used
1 bay leaf
salt and pepper
½ lb (225g) button mushrooms

Cut the fillet in half and coat each piece with plain flour. Melt the butter in a frying pan. Place the coated fillets in the pan and fry until golden brown on both sides. Place the meat, tomato sauce, stock, bay leaf and a little salt and pepper in a casserole dish. Cover and bake for 1 hour at 180°C/350°F/gas mark 5. Prepare the mushrooms and add to the mixture in the casserole. Taste and add more salt and pepper if necessary. Bake for a further hour. Remove the bay leaf. Serve with a crisp green salad.

Puddings and Sweet Recipes
Ryseitiau Melysfwyd

Fruit Pudding
Pwdin Brith

A good standby for those times when you can't think what to have for dessert, or you have some suet that you want to use up. Remember – Welsh women never wasted anything at all!

6 ozs (175g) self-raising flour
3 ozs (75g) granulated sugar
1½ ozs (38g) suet
1 level teaspoon mixed spice
4 ozs (125g) mixed dried fruit
¾ pint (175ml) milk

Prepare a heatproof basin by greasing it with a little margarine. Sieve the flour and mixed spice, mix in the suet, sugar and dried fruit. Add enough milk to form a soft consistency. Pour into the prepared basin, cover with a lid or foil. Steam for 2 – 2½ hours. Serve with white sauce or custard.

Christmas Pudding
Pwdin Dolig

**My favourite of all puddings. My mother never measured anything
when cooking, it was a pinch of this and a cupful of that. Her
Christmas puddings were always dark, rich and fantastic.**

2 ozs (50g) suet

2 ozs (50g) self-raising flour

4 ozs (125g) breadcrumbs

pinch of salt

4 ozs (125g) dark brown sugar

3 ozs (75g) currants

3 ozs (75g) raisins

3 ozs (75g) sultanas

2 ozs (50g) candied peel

2 eggs

1 tablespoon treacle

¼ pint (150ml) milk

1 level teaspoon mixed spice

½ level teaspoon ground ginger

Sieve the flour, salt and spices into a large bowl. Mix in the breadcrumbs, dried
fruit, sugar and suet. Add the beaten eggs, treacle and enough milk to form a
soft consistency. Place in a heatproof basin, cover with a lid or foil. Steam for 3
hours, and then for 1 hour on Christmas Day. Do not allow to boil dry. Serve
with your favourite sauce.

Snowdon Pudding
Pwdin Yr Wyddfa

Snowdon is popular with visitors and I understand that this dessert was prepared for them during Victorian times. There are two types of Snowdon Pudding, each with a white top. This is the version that I like best.

Pudding:
¾ pint (400ml) milk
2 ozs (50g) butter
3 ozs (75g) breadcrumbs
2 ozs (50g) caster sugar
grated rind of 1 lemon
Topping:
2 eggs
1 oz (25g) marmalade
2 ozs (50g) caster sugar

Put the butter and milk in a pan and bring to the boil. Pour over the breadcrumbs, sugar and lemon rind, mix well and leave to cool. Beat the egg yolks and mix in. Pour into a prepared baking dish. Bake at 180°C/350°F/gas mark 5 for 30 minutes or until set.

For the topping, whisk the egg whites and add the caster sugar, then whisk again to form a stiff meringue. Spread a layer of marmalade on the pudding and pile the meringue on top to form peaks. Bake in a cool oven for about 30 minutes or until the meringue is crisp and brown.

Raglan Pudding
Pwdin Rhaglan

This pudding always reminds me of the 'medelwyr' – harvesters of olden times. Welsh people used to make an annual trek to the Welsh border farms around Hereford in July and August, then return to work on their own harvest in September.

6 ozs (175g) self-raising flour

pinch of salt

2 eggs

½ pint (300ml) milk

2 ozs (50g) butter

1lb (450g) prepared fruit: apples, pears, plums or blackberries

½ teaspoon mixed spice

4 ozs (125g) caster or soft brown sugar

Sieve the flour and salt, beat into a smooth batter with the eggs and half of the milk. Add the rest of the milk slowly. Put the butter in a baking tin (10" x 12"/25 cm x 30 cm) and place in a hot oven for 1 minute or until the butter melts. Put the prepared fruit in the tin, cover with the sugar and spice. Pour the batter over and bake in a hot oven at 220°C/425°F/gas mark 7 for 30 minutes, reducing the heat to 180°C/350°F/gas mark 5 for a further 20–30 minutes. Serve warm with fresh double cream.

Summer Pudding
Pwdin yr Haf

Welsh women have always made full use of the wild blackberries that grow in abundance, just waiting to be collected. This is a lovely way of using them.

1 lb (450g) fresh soft fruits: raspberries, blackcurrants or blackberries
sugar to taste
thin slices of white bread – sliced bread is ideal

Prepare the fruit and simmer gently with the sugar and a little water. Place layers of bread and fruit alternately in a bowl, starting and ending with a layer of bread. Cover with a plate and place a heavy weight on it, such as a bag of sugar. Leave overnight and then turn onto a serving dish. Serve with fresh single cream.

Blackcurrant Cheesecake
Cacen Gaws Cwrens Duon

When I was young I was always given the task of topping and tailing blackcurrants. There were plenty growing in my grandmother's garden as in everyone else's garden. I hated the job, but loved the dishes made from them.

3 ozs (75g) butter
6 ozs (175g) crushed digestive biscuits
I level teaspoon gelatine
juice of one lemon
8 ozs (225g) cottage cheese, sieved
5 fl ozs (150ml) soured cream
3 ozs (75g) caster sugar
2 eggs, separated
I tin of blackcurrant pie filling or 1lb (450g) prepared blackcurrants cooked gently in sugar and left to go cold

Melt the butter and mix with the biscuit crumbs. Press the mixture onto the bottom of a 7" (18 cm) flan or pie dish. Sprinkle the gelatine into 4 teaspoons of cold water in a small bowl. Place the bowl in a pan of hot water and stir the gelatine until it dissolves. Put the lemon juice, cottage cheese, soured cream and sugar in a bowl and mix together. Add the egg yolks and gelatine, stirring continuously. Whisk the egg white and fold in gently. Pour into the flan case. Cool overnight and then cover with the blackcurrant mixture.

Gooseberry Cream
Ceuled Eirin Mair

Like blackcurrants, there were always plenty of gooseberries to be prepared, but I got through the topping and tailing much quicker.

I lb (450g) gooseberries
2 tablespoons water
4 ozs (125g) sugar
¼ pint (150ml) double cream
I level tablespoon custard powder
I level tablespoon caster sugar
¼ pint (150ml) milk

Top and tail the gooseberries and put them in a pan with the sugar. Cook until soft and put through a sieve to form a purée. Mix the custard powder and caster sugar to make a paste with a little of the milk, then boil the rest of the milk. Pour the milk onto the mixture and stir well. Return to the pan and cook until the mixture has thickened. Leave to cool, stirring occasionally. Stir in the purée and cream. Divide between four sundae dishes and chill before serving.

Rhubarb Tart
Tarten Riwbob

Welsh women used to have a baking day each week – 'diwrnod pobi'. My mother baked on Fridays and always made two or three fruit tarts amongst other things. An apple tart was made and saved for Sunday and the other tarts would be made from any fruit that was in season, or she would use bottled fruit.

8 ozs (225g) plain flour
4 ozs (125g) lard
pinch of salt
water
1½ lbs (675g) prepared rhubarb, cut into 1" (2.5 cm) pieces
10 ozs (300g) sugar
2 level tablespoons cornflour
8 ozs (225g) cream cheese
2 eggs
whipping cream

Add the salt to the flour and rub in the fat, adding enough water to make a dough. Line an 8" (20 cm) flan case with it and bake blind at 180°C/350°F/gas mark 5 for 20-30 minutes. Place the fruit, 8 ozs (225g) sugar, cornflour and a little water in a pan and cook gently until the mixture thickens, stirring continuously. Leave to cool and pour into the flan case. Beat the eggs, add the cream cheese and the rest of the sugar. Mix together and pour over the rhubarb mixture. Bake at 180°C/350°F/gas mark 5 for 30 minutes. Can be served cold with whipped cream.

Buttermilk Pancake
Crempog Llaeth Enwyn

Buttermilk was one of the basic foods for the poor in olden times – just think of the extra calcium it gave them! I love pancakes and this is my favourite recipe.

8 ozs (225g) plain flour
3 ozs (75g) sugar
½ pint (300 ml) buttermilk
1 egg
1 level teaspoon baking powder
1 level teaspoon bicarbonate of soda
lard or oil to cook

Sieve the flour, baking powder and bicarbonate of soda together into a large bowl. Add the sugar and mix well. Beat the egg and add with the buttermilk to the flour mixture. Beat well with a wooden spoon for a good 5 minutes. Let the mixture stand for 1–2 hours. Melt a little lard or oil in a skillet or heavy frying pan. When it is hot, pour a good tablespoonful of the mixture in. When the sides start to crinkle, turn the pancake over. Serve hot with butter.

Toffee
Taffi/Cyfleth

Making 'cyfleth' was a favourite pastime in lonely Welsh cottages on cold winter evenings. This was my mother's remedy for a cough.

8 ozs (225g) sugar
3 tablespoons treacle
2 ozs (50g) butter

Melt the butter gently in a heavy saucepan. Add the treacle and sugar. Stir gently over a low heat until the mixture forms a liquid. Bring slowly to the boil. Boil for 5 minutes or until a drop forms a soft ball in cold water. Pour into a greased tin and cool overnight.

Gwenlli Pudding
Pwdin Gwenlli

In one cookery book I read:
"Eggs are essential as a standby. They often save the situation in an emergency."

This was probably true in olden days also, when eggs were cheap and plentiful. Most women who had a large garden kept hens, especially during the war years. In those days, all hens were 'free range'.

3 large eggs
2 ozs (50g) granulated sugar
2 drops vanilla essence
½ pint (300ml) milk
1 packet powdered gelatine
2 tablespoons (30ml) hot water
3 ozs (75g) brown breadcrumbs
½ pint (300ml) whipping cream

Whisk the eggs. Put the sugar, vanilla essence and milk in a pan and heat gently until the sugar is dissolved. Add the eggs, bring to the boil and stir until thick custard has formed. Dissolve the gelatine in the hot water. Add the dissolved gelatine and the breadcrumbs to the custard. Stir lightly and pour into a mould. Leave to set. Serve with the whipped cream.

Conway Strawberries
Mefus Conwy

Most of the houses in the village where I was born and raised had gardens in which soft fruit grew. However, I cannot recall anyone growing strawberries. The only ones I had when I was little were ones from a tin. This is a lovely, easy recipe.

1lb (450g) fresh strawberries
4 ozs (100g) caster sugar
1 packet powdered gelatine
¼ pint (150ml) hot water
½ pint (300ml) double cream

Hull the strawberries and wash. Place in a large basin, mash them a little with a fork and sprinkle the caster sugar over them. Leave to stand for 2–3 hours and then rub the mixture through a coarse sieve. Dissolve the gelatine in the hot water. Whip the cream until stiff, and then add the fruit and dissolved gelatine. Mix well. Pour into four individual glass dishes and leave in a cool place to set.

Cake Recipes
Ryseitiau Teisen

Grandmother's Honey Cake
Teisen Fêl Nain

Honey was very often used as a sweetener in the olden days as sugar was so expensive. My grandmother used it for cooking and as a medicine.

Cake:
8 ozs (225g) plain flour
½ teaspoon bicarbonate of soda
1 teaspoon ground cinnamon
4 ozs (125g) butter or margarine
4 ozs (125g) brown sugar
2 eggs, separated
4 ozs (125g) soft honey, warmed

Topping:
2 ozs (50g) caster sugar
1 tablespoon soft honey, warmed

Sieve the flour, bicarbonate of soda and cinnamon. In another bowl, cream the fat and sugar until light and fluffy. Beat in the egg yolks and honey. Fold in the flour mixture and add a little warm water if necessary to keep the mixture soft. Beat one of the egg whites and fold into the mixture. Place in a round 7" (18 cm), well-greased cake tin and bake at 200°C/400°F/gas mark 6 for 15 minutes. Lower the heat to 180°C/350°F/gas mark 5 for 20 – 30 minutes, until the cake has risen and is golden brown. Remove from the oven, leave to cool a little and take out of the cake tin. Beat the other egg white until stiff and add the caster sugar. Brush the top of the cake with warm honey. Cover with the meringue and place back in the oven for 5 – 10 minutes until the top is golden brown. It is delicious when eaten while still warm.

Buttermilk Loaf
Torth Llaeth Enwyn

A cake with an old-fashioned flavour.

8 ozs (225g) plain flour
I teaspoon baking powder
pinch of salt
I level teaspoon cinnamon
4 ozs (125g) butter
4 ozs (125g) soft brown sugar
2 eggs
¼ pint (150 ml) buttermilk

Sieve the flour, baking powder, salt and cinnamon. Cream the fat and sugar and add the beaten eggs a little at a time. Fold in the flour mixture and mix well. Add the buttermilk and a little water if necessary to form a soft, dropping consistency. Pour into a prepared 1lb (450g) loaf tin and bake at 180°C/350°F/gas mark 5 for 30 to 45 minutes, or until risen and golden brown. It is delicious hot or cold.

Speckled Bread
Bara Brith

A couple of years ago I decided to sort out my recipes. I was tired of tatty bits of paper with recipes on them falling out of my cookery books. When I had collected them together I discovered that two-thirds of them were for Bara Brith – need I say more about this popular loaf?

1¼ lbs (675g) plain white flour
1 level teaspoon salt
1 oz (25g) lard
¼ teaspoon mixed spice
8 ozs (225g) currants
2 ozs (50g) chopped candied peel
½ oz (13g) yeast
¾ pint (600ml) warm milk
1 level teaspoon caster sugar

Sieve the flour, add the salt and rub in the fat. Mix in the spice, currants and peel. Cream the yeast with the sugar and add to the milk. Make a well in the flour, pour in the liquid and sprinkle a little of the flour mixture on top of the liquid. Cover with a warm damp cloth and leave to rise in a warm place for 30 minutes. Mix into a stiff dough, cover and leave to rise again in a warm place for 1 hour or until it has doubled in size.

Divide the dough in half, knead it a little and place in two well-greased 1lb (450g) bread tins. Leave in a warm place to rise again for 30 mintues. Place in a hot oven for 10 minutes at 230°C/450°F/gas mark 8 and then reduce the heat to 180°C/350°F/gas mark 5 and bake for a further 30 to 45 minutes.

Harvest Cake
Teisen y Cynhaeaf

Harvest was a very busy time for the farmer's wife with all the extra cooking and baking for friends and neighbours who came to help. This cake was quick to prepare and delicious eaten hot or cold.

6 ozs (175g) butter or margarine

2 eggs

6 ozs (175g) granulated sugar

8 ozs (225g) self-raising flour

pinch of salt

3 ozs (75g) soft brown sugar

2 ozs (50g) sultanas

1 oz (25g) chopped nuts

½ teaspoon cinnamon

1 lb (450g) cooking apples – peeled and cut into small pieces

Melt the fat and pour into a bowl. Add the beaten eggs, sugar, flour and salt and beat well. In another bowl mix the brown sugar, sultanas, nuts, cinnamon and apples. Grease a round, loose-bottomed, 7" (18 cm) cake tin and pour in half the batter. Add the fruit mixture, spreading it evenly. Cover with the rest of the batter. Bake at 180°C/350°F/gas mark 5 for an hour or until firm and golden brown.

Bakestone Cake
Teisen Lap

A firm Welsh favourite.

8 ozs (225g) plain flour
2 teaspoons baking powder
½ teaspoon nutmeg
2 ozs (50g) butter
2 ozs (50g) lard
4 ozs (125g) mixed dried fruit
4 ozs (125g) soft brown sugar
2 eggs, beaten
¼ pint (150ml) single cream or buttermilk

Sieve the flour, baking powder and nutmeg into a mixing bowl. Rub the fat in until the mixture looks like fine breadcrumbs. Add the fruit and sugar and mix well, adding the eggs and cream, or buttermilk, to form a soft, dropping consistency. Place in a well-greased shallow tin or on an enamel plate. Bake at 180°C/350°F/gas mark 5 for 30 minutes then reduce the heat and bake at 100°C/200°F/gas mark 3 for a further 30-35 minutes. Serve warm.

Welsh Cakes
Cacennau Cri/Pice ar y Maen

There is only one fault with these lovely little cakes – they are eaten as soon as they are baked!

8 ozs (225g) self-raising flour
¼ teaspoon mixed spice
2 ozs (50g) butter
2 ozs (50g) lard
3 ozs (75g) caster sugar
2 ozs (50g) currants
I egg, beaten
2-3 tablespoons milk

Sieve the flour and spice into a bowl, rub the fat into the flour, add the sugar and currants. Mix well and add the egg and enough milk to form a stiff dough. Roll out onto a floured board to ¼" (5 mm) thick. Cut into rounds and bake on a hot, greased griddle until golden brown on both sides. Dust with caster sugar. Wonderful when eaten hot or cold.

Oat Crunchies
Teisennau Ceirch

Ideal with a cup of coffee.

6 ozs (175g) plain flour
1oz (25g) oats
pinch of salt
2 level teaspoons baking powder
1 level teaspoon mixed spice
2 ozs (50g) margarine
2 ozs (50g) sugar
3 tablespoons golden syrup

Sieve the flour, salt, baking powder and mixed spice into a mixing bowl. Rub in the margarine, add the sugar and oats. Warm the syrup and mix in to make a stiff dough. Form the mixture into small balls – about 16. Place well spaced on a greased baking sheet and bake at 200°C/400°F/gas mark 6 for about 8 minutes. Remove from the tray while still warm.

Brecon Fingers
Bysedd Brycheiniog

I love oats – there is nothing that I like better than a bowlful of porridge and I use oats for cooking whenever possible. Oats was one of the basic foods of the Welsh for hundreds of years.

6 ozs (175g) chopped dates
3 tablespoons honey
8 tablespoons water
2 tablespoons lemon juice
2 level teaspoons plain flour
4 ozs (125g) brown sugar
4 ozs (125g) self-raising flour
5 ozs (150g) oats
6 ozs (175g) butter or margarine, melted

Grease a 7" (18cm) square baking tin. Put the dates and honey in a pan, add the lemon juice, plain flour and water. Bring to the boil, cook gently for 5 minutes. Leave to cool. Mix the self raising flour, sugar, oats and butter. Spread half of this mixture onto the prepared tin and press down well. Cover with the date mixture and spread the rest of the crumble mixture on top. Press down well. Bake at 180°C/350°F/gas mark 5 for 20 – 30 minutes or until golden brown. When cool, cut into fingers.

Miser's Cake
Teisen y Cybydd

I don't know why it is called 'Teisen y Cybydd'; maybe because it seems to last longer as it needs to mature to obtain the best flavour.

8 ozs (225g) plain flour
3 ozs (75g) oatmeal
¼ teaspoon bicarbonate of soda
¼ pint (150ml) milk
4 ozs (125g) treacle
4 ozs (125g) golden syrup
1 level teaspoon ground ginger
2 ozs (50g) margarine

Grease a 9" (23 cm) square cake tin. Mix all the dry ingredients and dissolve the soda in the milk. Melt the treacle, syrup, milk mixture and margarine together and add to the dry ingredients. Beat the mixture well and pour into the prepared tin. Bake at 180°C/350°F/gas mark 5 for 45 minutes. When cold, store in an airtight container for at least 3 days, then cut into squares.

Ginger Biscuits
Bisgedi Sinsir

**Lovely – they can also be made into gingerbread men, if you have
plenty of time. Ginger was very often used for flavouring in the past.
It has the kind of taste that reminds you of childhood.**

2 ozs (50g) butter
4 ozs (125g) caster sugar
1 egg
4 ozs (125g) plain flour
1 level teaspoon ground ginger
¼ teaspoon bicarbonate of soda
pinch of salt
a little milk

Cream the butter and sugar and mix in the rest of the ingredients, adding a
little milk if necessary to form a stiff dough. Place in the refrigerator for
2–3 hours. Roll out to ⅛"(0.3cm) thickness and cut into rounds with a plain
cutter. Bake on a greased baking sheet at 180°C/350°F/gas mark 5 for 15–20
minutes. Leave to cool.

Orange Loaf
Torth Oren

My mother never used a cookery book, although she did have one. It was a wedding present, and I have it now. There is no date on it, but I think that it must have been printed around 1937, the year my parents were married. It is interesting to read because all the ingredients used are priced. For example, 2 lbs of butter was one shilling (5p)! Try this recipe from the book.

1 large or 2 medium oranges
5 ozs (150g) butter
6 ozs (175g) granulated sugar
3 large eggs
8 ozs (225g) self-raising flour

Grease and line a 1lb (450g) loaf tin. Grate the rind of the orange and extract the juice. Cream the butter and sugar until soft. Whisk the eggs and add to the mixture, a little at a time. Sieve the flour and gently fold into the mixture. Add the rind and juice, mix well and add a little water, if necessary, to obtain a soft, dropping consistency. Pour into the prepared tin. Bake at 180°C/ 350°F/gas mark 5 for 1 hour or until golden brown.

– Wales within your reach:
an attractive series
at attractive prices!

Titles already published:

1. Welsh Talk
Heini Gruffudd
086243 447 5
£2.95

2. Welsh Dishes
Rhian Williams
086243 492 0
£2.95

3. Welsh Songs
Lefi Gruffudd (ed.)
086243 525 0
£3.95

4. Welsh Mountain Walks
Dafydd Andrews
086243 547 1
£3.95

To be published soon:

5. Welsh Place Names
Iain Ó hAnnaidh
086243 514 5
£4.95

6. Welsh Castles
Geraint Roberts
086243 550 1
£3.95

7. Welsh Railways
Jim Green
086243 551 X
£3.95

8. Welsh Rugby Heroes
Androw Bennett
086243 552 8
£3.95

The *It's Wales* series
is just one of a wide range
Welsh interest publications
from Y Lolfa.
For a full list of books currently in print,
send now for your free copy
of our new, full-colour Catalogue
– or simply surf into our website
at **www.ylolfa.com**.

Talybont Ceredigion Cymru/*Wales* SY24 5AP
ffôn 0044 (0)1970 832 304 *ffacs* 832 782 *isdn* 832 813
e-bost ylolfa@ylolfa.com *y we* www.ylolfa.com